Quick and easy recipes to in

# Deliciously
# Healthy 2

**FREE FROM**
Dairy
Wheat
Refined sugar
Unfermented soya

# JULIE HARRISON

# CONTENTS

# INTRODUCTION

My first recipe book Deliciously Healthy has changed people's lives, and I hope to do the same with Deliciously Healthy 2. So often I hear the words "I don't have time to make healthy food", "Healthy food is for rabbits!" and "My family hate healthy dishes". It doesn't have to be like that, and that's why I created my recipe books. If you want some very quick easy super tasty, but above all healthy food, you've picked the right book.

Back in 2009, I thought I was eating a healthy diet – I was certainly following government guidelines, but then I found out I had breast cancer. I had surgery but started to find out the health benefits of eating a more natural diet and changing my lifestyle. So much so that by the time I had recovered from my operation I had the courage to say that I didn't want any more conventional treatment, so I refused chemotherapy, radiotherapy and all drugs. It was certainly very scary, but it also felt right. I figured out what to do all by myself, without any real mentors or guides, just huge amounts of research and study. I started to eliminate certain food groups I never thought I would be able to let go. Dairy and refined sugars are the two best examples and ones I still avoid today, many years later.

If you've bought my first book, I'd like to say a big "Thank you" to you because without you this book wouldn't have been created. My readers are very important to me, and I want to stop the confusion about what's healthy and what's not. There is a minefield of information out in the world, and I'll make the journey easier for you.

I urge you to read the following pages, which most people skip through before the recipes. You will gain more understanding as to why certain ingredients are used as well as lots of time-saving solutions.

WARNING
There are a lot of chocolate based recipes. The reason? Raw cacao has many health benefits. It's the dairy and refined sugar that are usually added that make it unhealthy. It tastes divine too!

# INGREDIENTS

All of my creations are dairy, wheat, refined sugar and unfermented soya free. If you want to find out why I chose not to eat these foods, then please read one of my other books 'From Cancer to Clear - my eight eye openers to improve your health' which is available on Amazon. In that book, I explain my journey from being diagnosed with breast cancer to complete recovery and my eye openers which will help improve anyone's health, in easy, simple steps.

Most of my recipes are suitable for vegans, but I do eat a small amount of grass-fed organically reared meat. Almost everything I eat and drink is grown or raised to organic standards, but I'm not ruled by something having a label. I use my judgment and instinct and try to eat locally wherever possible. It really is worth doing some initial research to check out your local suppliers. Most will be delighted that you care about the way they produce their food. Make friends with your grocer, butcher and health store owner. If you buy organic food, you are almost guaranteed it isn't genetically modified. Should you think that GM crops are a good idea, I would urge you to spend some time on the internet and explore the issue. The Soil Association is a good place to start.

I adore coconut oil and use it all the time for cooking. If you don't like it, then you can use any vegetable oil. However, if you are trying to improve your health, cold pressed oils are the ones to use. Avoid heating them because the molecular structure changes and they become toxic.

Food should be unprocessed and as close to coming out of the ground as possible. Nowadays almost all the food in your local supermarket should be considered fake food, as it has been processed in some way, resulting in severely depleted nutrients. That is why I try to avoid supermarkets where possible, and instead, have my food delivered from local organic companies.

If you can, buy in bulk because the savings can be quite substantial. I have a bookcase I use for a backup store of staple ingredients. Sometimes it feels like I am playing at "shop". On the next few pages are some suggestions for store cupboard staples. You certainly don't need all of them to make my recipes, but they are a good starting point.

# STORE CUPBOARD STAPLES

I would really consider investing in organic where possible for your ingredients, but especially your herbs and spices because they have such a powerful effect on the body and you want to ensure the best effect. In my opinion, meat should be grass fed and reared to organic standards. Check out the Dirty Dozen List on page 5 and see where you can save money on your fruit and vegetables.

## Ingredients

This is a very basic list, and you will probably add to it when you start creating new recipes. However, by having the majority of these items to hand means you can produce a wide variety of wonderfully healthy, nutritious and tasty meals.

**Herbs and Spices**
Herbs de Provence
Mixed herbs
Turmeric
Curry powder
Cumin powder
Corriander powder
Smoked paprika powder
Chilli powder
Fajita mix, see my recipe
Himalayan rock salt
Black peppercorns
Nutmeg
Mixed spice
Cinnamon

**Grains and Pulses**
Quinoa
Chickpeas, ideally dried
Aduki beans
Cannellini beans

Butter beans
Puy lentils
Oats
Rice flour
Gram flour (chickpea)
Buckwheat flour
Coconut flour
Cornflour
Arrowroot

**Nuts and seeds**
Whole raw almonds
Cashew nuts
Walnut pieces
Sunflower seeds
Chia seeds
Broccoli seeds (for sprouting)
Red clover seeds (for spouting)
China Rose radish seeds
(for sprouting)

# STORE CUPBOARD STAPLES

## Miscellaneous
Tamari soya sauce (wheat free)
Rice wine vinegar
Fish sauce
Miso
Apple cider vinegar with the mother
Mustard
Stock powder
Chilli sauce
Eggs
Sun-dried tomatoes
Passata
Rice pasta
Konjac noodles
Almond or peanut butter
Tomato paste
Coconut chips
Raw cacao powder
Raisins
Dried apricots
Dates
Unrefined cane sugar (for fermented drinks)
Coconut sugar
Date syrup
Maple syrup
Vanilla extract
Baking powder

## Oils
For heating only use coconut oil
Extra virgin olive oil
Toasted sesame oil
Unrefined cold pressed sesame oil

## Frozen Foods
Peas
Sweetcorn
Frozen berries
Fish
Chicken thighs
Chicken mince
Minced steak

## Fresh Vegetables & Fruit
White onions
Red onions
Peppers
Red or white cabbage
Carrots
Celery
Spinach
Watercress
Ginger
Garlic
Chilli
Avocado
Tomatoes
Cucumber
Lemons
Apples
Bananas
Any seasonal fruits
and vegetables

# THE DIRTY DOZEN

If possible buy organic items from the list below because they contain the highest level of pesticides.

## The Dirty Dozen

| | |
|---|---|
| Strawberries | Cherries |
| Spinach | Grapes |
| Nectarines | Celery |
| Apples | Tomatoes |
| Peaches | Sweet bell peppers |
| Pears | Potatoes |

## The Clean Fifteen

The next list has relatively low levels of pesticides, so if you are trying to save money, these are a safer option. It is often called the Clean Fifteen List.

| | |
|---|---|
| Sweetcorn | Mangos |
| Avocados | Aubergine |
| Pineapples | Honeydew melon |
| Cabbage | Kiwi |
| Onions | Cantaloupe melon |
| Sweet peas (frozen) | Cauliflower |
| Papayas | Grapefruit |
| Asparagus | |

If you base your choices on these two lists, you will reduce your pesticide level by around 70%.

Each year the Environmental Working Group produce an updated list. Check my website for the latest list.

# EQUIPMENT

I love my gadgets, and over the years I've bought lots to speed up the time spent in the kitchen. However, I've tried to create most of my recipes with the minimum of equipment. A good sharp kitchen knife and a stick blender will get you by for most recipes. I used to use a Vitamix and then an Omniblend, but Ninja has created my all-time kitchen gadget which is the Ninja Ultimate Chopper, Blender & Mini Food Processor - NN100UK. It's amazing value for money and has replaced a number of my gadgets and no, I'm not on commission!

Scales aren't necessary either, but a set of measuring cups and spoons would be very useful. If you don't have any then 1 cup is equal to 250 ml of liquid. Dried weights vary so find a container that holds 250 ml of liquid, and you can use that to work out the dried amounts. A teaspoon holds 5 ml of liquid, so therefore you can use the same principle as for the cups.

I have assumed a certain level of competence in the kitchen, but even complete beginners shouldn't have a problem because all of my recipes are very forgiving. Just taste as you go. By using natural ingredients, you are never 100% sure how something will turn out so adjust the ingredients to suit your taste.

On the following page, you will find my 'essential' and my 'wishlist' items.

# ESSENTIAL AND WISH LIST OF EQUIPMENT

You can spend a fortune on kitchen gadgets, and I have over the years, but learn from my mistakes and save money. Most of us are on a budget and space can be an issue too. I suggest leaving your equipment out on the work counter because otherwise, you won't use it as much, it's just human nature.

My first list is what I consider my essential equipment that you will need to produce healthy tasty food in a short space of time. My second "wishlist" includes items that are nice to have if your finances and space allow. My lists are just starting points of course, and yours will vary.

**Essential**
Chopping boards
Sharp kitchen knife
Vegetable peeler
Grater
Measuring cups
Measuring spoons
Wooden spoon
Spatula
Large plastic bowl
Glass jam jars
Tin opener
Selection of bowls
Stick blender
Large sauté pan with lid
Small saucepan with lid
Large saucepan with lid
Roasting tray
Loaf tin
Square 8" cake tin
Loose bottom round cake tin
Jug water filter

**Wish List**
Large stainless steel bowl
Potato masher
Fish slice
Hand whisk
Soup ladle
Tongs
Measuring jug
Wooden pounder
Rolling pin
Garlic crusher
Ice lolly moulds
Cooling rack
Sprouting trays
Mason jars & bottles
Mandoline slicer
Metal sieve
Plastic sieve
Colander
Lemon squeezer
Bottle opener
Timer

Salad spinner
Multi-purpose cooker (InstantPot) or
Slow cooker
Pressure cooker
Casserole dish
Large salad bowl
Carving knife
Probe thermometer
Small frying pan
Large frying pan
Scales
Kettle
Toaster
Juicer
Spirilizer
Ninja (NN100UK)
Steamer
Dehydrator

# YOUR WEEKLY
# FOOD SHOP

Leave behind the mindset of shopping in a supermarket once or twice a week if you want to shop effectively. You will end up buying things you don't need and be tempted by the convenience food that is so prevalent. Instead, get as much delivered to your door as possible. I like to use a local organic supplier of vegetables and meat plus a whole food co-operative for my store cupboard essentials. If I were buying in smaller quantities, I would be using my local independent health food store when I'm in town. I do use my local supermarket, but it's not for my main shopping and certainly not every week.

I split food into 3 categories; fresh, frozen and store cupboard staples.
Fresh food is mainly fruit and vegetables which I suggest you buy from your local organic producer or use one of the many online companies that deliver your supplies on a weekly basis. Research and find out if your local butcher has organic, grass fed meat or again order online.

Store cupboard staples can be purchased either from your local health food store or online. Order larger quantities from wholesale companies if your funds and storage facilities allow which will save you more money in the long run. The aim is to keep extra spare items that you use frequently. Keep a list of items that are getting low and order before you run out.

Hopefully, you are starting to see that with a little bit of planning and organisation you can really simplify the whole process of your "weekly" shop. Visits to the supermarket will be less frequent, and you will have the satisfaction of saving time and money, plus supporting ethical co-operatives or family firms. Supermarkets are quite often more expensive than small local stores.

# YOUR KITCHEN LAYOUT

Do you want to prepare your meals quickly and easily? If so you only need to have some basic items and good organisation; plus the raw ingredients of course. I used to be a minimalist in the kitchen. When I became serious about food preparation, I soon realised the error of my ways! If you put your gadgets away and keep your work surfaces clear then, you tend not to use them. I now leave virtually all of my equipment on the work surface, so they are always to hand.

I prepare almost everything in an area 80 cm x 40 cm, so don't let lack of space stop you. You really don't need a large area. By being restricted it means you have to clean and tidy as you go. There is nothing worse than having to clear up everything at the end which is what often happens if you use lots of work surfaces.

Your work area is best being near your sink, ideally with your fridge close by too. I suggest keeping all your dried ingredients in one cupboard with the things you use the most often on shelves within easy reach at the front. Always try to put things back in the same place, so you don't waste time rummaging around trying to find that elusive item.

Consider using a large storage box on a shelf for smaller items that you can fill neatly. You can then see at a glance what you have.

Avoid canned food and any containers with plastic linings, such as tetra packaging. The chances are they will be lined with BPA or some other equivalent. If you use tinned tomatoes, consider using tomato paste in a jar and/or passata. I do occasionally use canned foods, but whenever possible, I avoid them.

Equipment you use at least once a week should live out on your work surface, if possible. Any equipment you don't use very often can be stored in a cupboard, or ask yourself "Do you really need it?".

Keep all your saucepans in one place and even think about leaving your most used pans out on the cooker.

# YOUR KITCHEN LAYOUT

Buy a cutlery drawer tidy to keep your serving items together.

Keep your cups or mugs together with the hot drinks you consume in a cupboard by the kettle.

Consider storing knives on a magnetic strip close to your work area but out of harm's way. Try to keep them nice and sharp - blunt knives cause more accidents than sharp ones.

Your aim is to have everything you need to hand, in a logical order, to minimize time hunting for ingredients or equipment you know you have but can't find.

Hopefully, all these tips will seem like common sense, and you will wonder why it has taken you so long to sort out your kitchen.

# MY TOP TIPS

## Always Have a Well Stocked Store Cupboard

The secret to producing near effortless, delicious, nutritious and economical meals is to get organised. I have had decades of experience and pride myself in doing just that. By having a store cupboard full of essential ingredients, a fridge with the basics, a freezer stocked with some considered purchases and your new routine, you will be able to produce wonderful food in super quick time.

You will need to buy my list of store cupboard essentials but obviously omit any you hate or have intolerances to. You should never eat anything you really hate – it is usually your body's way of telling you something. Likewise, listen when you have a craving for something, although if you crave sugar all the time that is usually a sign you have excessive candida.

See page 3 for a list of ingredients you will need.

## Organise Your Kitchen

See 'Your Kitchen Layout' section, page 9, so you can make the best use of your space. You will be surprised just what you can achieve in a small area.

## Organise Your Fridge

Keep your lovely greens, salad and fruit on the shelves where you can see them rather than in the drawer at the bottom of your fridge. This way, whenever you open the door, you will be reminded to add a salad to your meal.

Make sure you deal with dirty dishes and keep the area clean and tidy as you go. There is usually time while your food is cooking. Your kitchen needs to become a welcoming space, one where you want to spend time.

# MY TOP TIPS

## Get Everything You Need Out Before You Start

Once you get into the habit of doing this life suddenly becomes much easier. You don't forget to add the odd ingredient or get halfway through a recipe and realise you don't have that vital item, although most things can be substituted.

## Get Ahead

Chilli, curries, stews, soups are examples of meals you should always cook in bulk. Store in the fridge and eat the day after next, so you aren't eating the same meal twice in a row. Alternatively, freeze portions, so you always have a selection; just make sure you clearly label your container together with the date.

When you unpack your vegetables, don't pile them in the fridge. Take the time to wash the salad leaves and greens, then spin them dry in a salad spinner. This means you only have to wash them once instead of every time you want a salad.

If you crave snacks, then prepare some chopped vegetables, fruit and hummus or guacamole, so they are ready and waiting for when you feel peckish. You will be less likely to cheat if you've got alternatives to hand.

## Keep Meals Simple

If you know you can produce a lovely meal within 30 minutes or less, then you are more likely to start, rather than reaching for the takeaway menu. Use my simple recipes and add in your old time favourites.

# ABOUT MY RECIPES

I've decided to split my recipes into 4 sections for this book - savoury, sweet, fermented and raw dishes. I'm still using the simplest of names so you can find your favourite recipes easily. Don't let this put you off; the tastes and flavours are wonderful. There is one exception which is my Juloaf. John, my wonderfully supportive boyfriend, suggested the name which is short for Julie's Loaf, I decided to humour him.

There is a complete list of my the recipes on page 16. The aim is to make my book as easy to use as possible. Be warned; there are a lot of chocolate based recipes. The reason, apart from the taste, is that raw cacao is so good for you. Almost all of my recipes are suitable for vegetarians except for four.

No food has been wasted in the creation of this recipe book. Nothing has been staged, and all the food was eaten for lunch or dinner. Each and every picture brings back memories to me of the time spent with my dear family and friends.

If you've got Deliciously Healthy, you might notice that some of the fermented recipes are called the same. However, during the last two years, I've simplified and improved them even further so that they're even easier to make and more delicious to eat.

There is just one recipe that is the same in both books, and that's my Fajita Mix. I've had so many people comment on it that I thought I would include it in my second book. Above all, enjoy creating, sharing and eating my healthy, tasty alternative recipes whilst knowing they are improving your health.

Please visit my website improveyourhealth.co.uk and 'like' my Facebook page to explore more about what I do and how I can help you. Sign up to my monthly mailing list on my website - each month I include my latest favourite recipe.

# RECIPE INDEX

## Raw Recipes

## Fermented Recipes

# LIST OF RECIPES

# ALMOND
# BUTTER FUDGE

Yield: 12 squares          Preparation Time: 10 minutes          Chill Time: 2 hours

## INGREDIENTS

12 Medjool dates stoned
1 cup almond butter
Salt

## METHOD

Line an 8" square container with baking parchment.

Process all the ingredients in a food processor until the dough turns into a ball.

Tip the mixture into the tin and press firmly down into the corners. I use damp hands.

Freeze for a couple of hours and then cut into squares.

Ideally, defrost for half an hour in your fridge before serving.

NOTES: *They will keep for a week in the fridge, or up to a month in a sealed container in the freezer.*

# APRICOT
# AND OAT SLICE

Yield: 12 slices          Preparation Time: 20 minutes          Cook Time: 35 minutes

## INGREDIENTS

1 1/2 cups dried apricots chopped

1 cup water

1/4 cup date syrup

3/4 cup coconut oil

1/2 cup desiccated coconut

2 cups oats processed into flour

1 cup oats

Salt

## METHOD

Pre-heat your oven to 200 C. Line an 8" square baking tin with greaseproof paper.

In a small saucepan add the chopped apricots and water and very gently simmer until the water is absorbed into the apricots. You only need a very gentle heat, and it will probably take about 10 minutes.

In a large mixing bowl add the date syrup and coconut oil. Gently melt over the pan of apricots (Bain Marie). Once melted remove from the pan.

Add the remaining ingredients to the date syrup and coconut oil then mix thoroughly. Press half into your baking tin ensuring that you press down really firmly or the mixture will crumble when you cut it. I use the palms of my damp hands.

Cover with the apricot mixture and then add the rest of the crumble mixture and press down firmly again.

Cook for 25 minutes. Allow to go cold on a rack and cut into 12 squares.

NOTES: *These keep for a week in an airtight tin. Gorgeous with a cup of delicate green tea.*

# BAKED FISH
# AND WEDGES

Yield: 4 portions          Preparation Time: 15 minutes          Cook Time: 40 minutes

## INGREDIENTS

### Sweet Potato Wedges
4 small sweet potatoes
6 tbsp melted coconut oil
1 tbsp turmeric
Salt and black pepper

### Baked Fish
1 cup desiccated coconut
1 cup almond flour
2 tbsp turmeric
1 tbsp garlic powder (optional)
2 tbsp mixed herbs
Salt and black pepper
2 eggs beaten
4 pieces of white fish
4 lemon wedges
Parsley to garnish

## METHOD

Preheat your oven to 200 C.
Line 2 baking trays with baking parchment or greaseproof paper.

### Sweet Potato Wedges

Cut your sweet potatoes into wedges leaving the skin on. Tip these onto one of the baking trays and coat with the coconut oil, turmeric and black pepper. Roast in the oven for about 40 minutes turning once halfway through. They should be golden brown.

### Baked Fish

Mix all the dry ingredients and tip onto a plate.

Coat the fish with the egg then dip in the coconut and almond mix pressing firmly into the fish. Place onto your 2nd lined baking tray.

Cook for about 15 minutes depending on the thickness of the fish.

Serve with the lemon wedges and garnish with parsley.

NOTES: *Delicious with salad and some fermented vegetables.*

# BAKED STUFFED BUTTERNUT SQUASH

Yield: 2 portions          Preparation Time: 10 minutes          Cook Time: 1 hour

## INGREDIENTS

1 butternut squash

2 tbsp coconut oil

1 small onion chopped

2 garlic cloves crushed

1 small chilli chopped

1 red pepper chopped

6 mushrooms chopped

1/2 cup cashew nut pieces

1 tbsp mixed herbs

1 tsp turmeric

Salt and black pepper

## METHOD

Preheat your oven to 180 C.

Cut the butternut squash in half, scoop out the seeds leaving as much flesh as possible. Rub the flesh with 1 tablespoon of the coconut oil.

Place in a roasting tin and bake upside down for between 30 - 45 minutes depending on its size.

In the meantime gently heat the rest of the coconut oil and saute the onions, garlic and chilli. Cover and allow to gently soften for about 10 minutes, stirring frequently.

Add the pepper, mushrooms, cashew nuts, herbs, spices, salt and pepper. Stir and cover for a further 5 minutes.

Check to see if your butternut squash is cooked (nice and soft), if it is, allow to cool slightly so you don't burn your hands. Very gently scoop out the flesh and add to the pan with the other vegetables. Mix thoroughly then pile back into the squash skins.

Return to the oven for 15 minutes.

**NOTES:** *Vary the stuffing mixture, try adding cooked beans, lentils or other vegetables. It's lovely cold with a salad too.*

# BLACKBERRY AND APPLE CRUMBLE

Yield: 4-6          Preparation Time: 15 minutes          Cook Time: 45 minutes

## INGREDIENTS

2 cups cooking apples chopped

2 cups blackberries or other berries

2 tbsp water

1/2 cup coconut oil

1/4 cup date syrup or another natural sweetener

1 1/2 cups oats

1/4 cup walnut pieces or other nuts

1/4 cup desiccated coconut

1/4 cup sunflower seeds

1/4 cup raisins

1/4 cup flax seeds

**NOTES:** *My crumble is lovely served warm but not too hot. Serve with homemade custard made with almond or other nut milk instead of cow's milk.*

## METHOD

Preheat your oven to 170 C.

In a saucepan add your chopped apples and blackberries with a couple of tablespoons of water, cover and very gently simmer for 5 minutes or until the apples have just started to soften. Stir frequently during this time. Taste, and if necessary add some natural sweetener or lemon juice. Transfer to an ovenproof dish.

Meanwhile, in a large bowl melt the coconut oil and mix in the date syrup over a pan of simmering water (Bain Marie). It will take just a couple of minutes to melt.

Remove from the heat and add in 3/4 cup of the oats (the other 3/4 cup will be processed into flour), nuts, coconut, seeds and raisins, mixing gently to combine.

In a food processor add the remaining 3/4 cup of oats and process into flour. Add to the oat mixture and mix together breaking up any big clumps. It should resemble a traditional crumble mix. Spoon the crumble mixture into your dish and gently press down into the fruit ensuring that all the apples and blackberries are covered.

Oven cook for 40 minutes, checking after 30 minutes and covering with greaseproof paper if it's browning too quickly.

# CANNELLINI AND PEPPER FAJITAS

Yield: 2 portions          Preparation Time: 10 minutes          Cook Time: 15 minutes

## INGREDIENTS

2 tbsp coconut oil

1/2 green pepper sliced

1/2 red pepper sliced

1/2 yellow pepper sliced

1 medium onion sliced

2 garlic cloves crushed

1 cup cannellini beans cooked

4 tbsp fajita mix (see my recipe page 50

## METHOD

Heat the coconut oil in a frying pan and sauté the onions and peppers for 5 minutes until just turning soft, stirring frequently.

Use a fork and break up the cannellini beans. Push the vegetables to the side of the pan then add the cannellini beans. Add the spice mixture, stir and cook for a further 5 minutes.

**NOTES:** *Serve in my Courgette Wraps with a lovely big salad.*

# CARROT GINGER AND CARDAMOM SALAD

Yield: 4 portions          Preparation Time: 10 minutes

## INGREDIENTS

4 medium carrots grated

3 spring onions finely sliced

1/2 cup fresh coriander chopped

1" ginger grated

1 lemon juiced

3 tbsp olive oil

5 cardamom pods

Salt and black pepper

## METHOD

Mix all the ingredients except the cardamom pods, salt and pepper.

Crush the cardamom pods to release the seeds and grind until fine.

Add to the salad and if necessary add the salt and pepper to taste.

**NOTES:** *This salad is really lovely with a curry and balances the fiery flavours.*

# CASHEW CRUSTED CHICKPEA BURGERS

Yield: 4 portions          Preparation Time: 15 minutes          Cook Time: 25 minutes

## INGREDIENTS

1 cup dried chickpeas
1 tbsp coconut oil
1/3 cup cashew pieces
1 tsp turmeric
Black pepper
1 medium onion chopped
2 cloves garlic chopped
1 tsp cumin ground
1 tsp coriander ground
1/4 cup parsley chopped
1/2 tsp cayenne pepper
3 tbsp lemon juice
1 tsp salt
1/2 cup gram flour (chickpea)

## METHOD

Soak the chickpeas for a minimum of 10 hours or up to 24 hours in lots of water.
Preheat your oven to 180 C. Grease a small baking tray.

Add the cashew pieces, turmeric and black pepper to your food processor to make the cashew crust. Pulse a few times to crush the nuts. Tip onto a plate. Don't wash your food processor just yet.

Drain the chickpeas, rinse and add them to your food processor with the spices, salt and blend until the mixture resembles fine breadcrumbs.

Add the onions, parsley, flour and lemon juice. Process again.

Wet your hands and form into 8 flattened balls, about one centimetre in height. Coat the burgers with the cashew crust mixture pressing the nuts gently into the surface.

Place on your greased baking tray and cook in the oven for 15 minutes. Turn and continue cooking for another 10 minutes.

NOTES: *These freeze beautifully uncooked. Defrost before cooking. They are also just as nice cold chopped up in a salad.*

# CHICKEN AND ADUKI BEAN THAI BURGERS

Yield: 4 portions          Preparation Time: 10 minutes          Cook Time: 15 minutes

## INGREDIENTS

1 cup aduki beans cooked

1 small red onion chopped

250g chicken mince

Handful of coriander chopped

1 tsp turmeric

1 tsp fish sauce (optional)

1/2 tsp rice vinegar

1/2 tsp salt

1 tbsp coconut oil

## METHOD

Add the aduki beans and onions to your food processor and pulse a few times to chop them together. Add the remaining ingredients and pulse a few times until everything is well combined. It should still have some texture.

Dampen your hands and form into 12 little patties. If you have time pop in your fridge for 20 minutes to firm up, but this step isn't essential.

Gently heat the coconut oil in a frying pan. Fry the patties for a few minutes each side until cooked through.

NOTES: *Serve with my Thai Vegetables and Konjac Noodles.*
*These are lovely cold, and they freeze either uncooked or cooked. I like to add some chopped chilli into the mix.*

# CHICKEN THIGHS MARINATED IN HERBS AND SPICES

Yield: 4 portions          Preparation Time: 10 minutes          Cook Time: 1 hour

## INGREDIENTS

1/2 small red onion finely sliced

3 cloves of garlic crushed

3 tbsp olive oil

2 tbsp balsamic vinegar

1 tbsp maple syrup

1/2 lemon juiced

1 tsp mixed herbs

1/2 tsp turmeric

Pinch cayenne pepper (optional)

Salt and black pepper

2 chicken thighs

## METHOD

Add all the ingredients apart from the chicken into a bowl and whisk together.

Remove the skin from the chicken, score the meat and add to the marinade.

If you have time refrigerate for 12 hours but one hour will do.

Preheat the oven to 180 C and roast for about one hour until the meat is cooked and tender. The size of your thighs will dictate for how long.

**NOTES:** *Serve with a big salad, coleslaw and fermented vegetables.*

# CHICKPEA AND AUBERGINE CASSEROLE

Yield: 4 portions          Preparation Time: 15 minutes          Cook Time: 1 hour

## INGREDIENTS

3 tbsp coconut oil

2 medium onions chopped

10 garlic cloves crushed

1 chilli chopped (optional)

2 medium aubergines chopped
1" cubes

2 cups chickpeas cooked

1 3/4 cups passata

Salt and black pepper

## METHOD

Gently fry the chopped onion, garlic and chilli for about 10 minutes. Cover the pan, stirring occasionally to stop it from sticking.

Add the chopped aubergines and gently fry for a further few minutes. Stir occasionally.

Add the cooked chickpeas, passata, salt and pepper and gently simmer, covered for 20 minutes on a low heat.

**NOTES:** *Vary the vegetables and beans depending what you have in your fridge and cupboard.*

*This dish is actually nicer cold the next day after the flavours have had a chance to mingle. Make double the batch and freeze the extra portions.*

# CHOCOLATE
# AND BEAN CAKE

Yield: 8 portions          Preparation Time: 15 minutes          Cook Time: 25 minutes

## INGREDIENTS

### Ganache
1/2 block coconut cream (100g)
1/3 cup coconut oil
1 can coconut milk full-fat
1/3 cup date syrup
2 tsp vanilla extract
3/4 cup cocoa powder

### Cake
3 cups cannellini beans cooked
1 cup almond butter or peanut butter
1/2 bottle (340g) date or maple syrup
1/2 cup cocoa powder
Approximately 1/2 cup almond milk
1 tbsp baking powder
Salt

## METHOD

Preheat the oven to 180 C.

Line 2 x 7" round cake tins with baking parchment or greaseproof paper. Ensure you grease any parts of the tins that aren't lined. If you don't have 7" tins use what you have and vary the cooking time.

Gently melt the coconut cream and coconut oil in a bowl over a saucepan of simmering water (Bain Marie). Open the can of coconut milk and carefully scoop out the thick cream leaving the liquid at the bottom. You need one cup of the cream.

Remove the melted coconut cream and oil from the heat and add the date or maple syrup, vanilla extract and cocoa powder. Whisk in the thick coconut cream and leave to one side to cool down. It needs to be cold, not chilled.

In a food processor add all cake ingredients keeping back half of the almond milk and process until the batter is really smooth. Depending on your beans you may need to add some more of the almond milk. The mixture should be like an old-fashioned sponge cake.

*more -*

# CHOCOLATE AND BEAN CAKE

## METHOD CONTINUED

Spread the batter evenly into the two prepared tins by using a wet spatula.

Bake for between 25 - 30 minutes or until a toothpick comes out cleanly and the edges are a tiny bit brown.

Allow to cool for 10 minutes and remove from the tins and cool on wire rack.

Once the cakes are cold, sandwich 1/3 of the frosting between them, using the rest of the frosting on the top and sides to decorate the cake.

**NOTES:** *This is a really decadent cake, and you can freeze it in individual portions.*

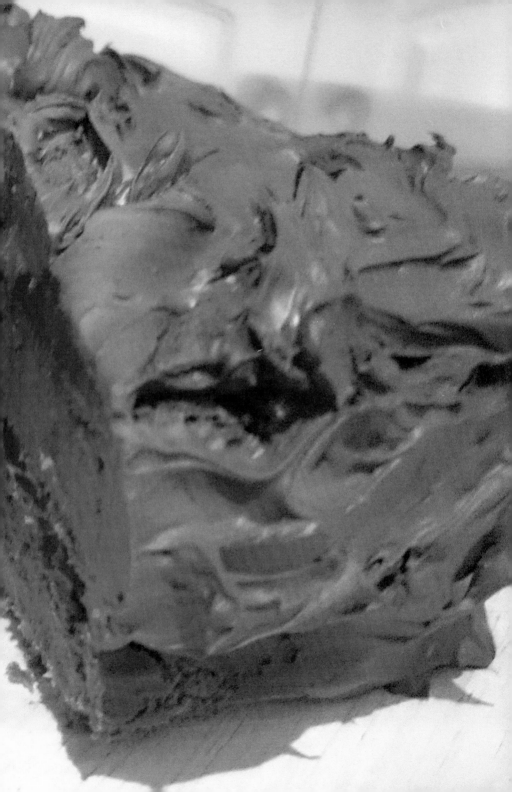

# CHOCOLATE AND COURGETTE MINI CUPCAKES

Yield: 24 mini cupcakes          Preparation Time: 20 minutes          Cook Time: 20 minutes

## INGREDIENTS

**Cupcake**

1 medium courgette roughly chopped

3/4 cup buckwheat flour

1 tbsp baking powder

3/4 cup dates chopped

2 really ripe bananas turning brown

1 can coconut milk full-fat

6 tbsp cocoa powder

**Frosting**

1 cup dates chopped soaked in boiling water 20 minutes

3 tbsp raw cacao

2 tsp vanilla extract

Salt

**Topping**

Pistachio nuts finely chopped

Goji berries finely chopped

## METHOD

Preheat the oven to 180 C. Line 2 x 12 mini 1" cupcake tins with cupcake liners.

Open the can of coconut milk and gently scoop out the cream. You need 3/4 cup of coconut cream and 1/4 cup of the coconut water for the cake mixture.

Add all the cupcake ingredients into a food processor and process until smooth.

Divide equally among the cupcake tins and bake for 20 minutes. Check that they are cooked by lightly pressing the surface - they should give slightly. If not, bake for another 5 minutes. Transfer to a rack to cool down.

Drain off the water from the dates reserving about 1/4 cup and add with all the frosting ingredients into your food processor and process until silky smooth.

When the cupcakes are completely cold, you can top with a spoonful of the frosting mixture. Decorate with the nuts and goji berries.

**NOTES:** *The cakes freeze really well or you can keep them for a couple of days in the fridge.*

# CHOCOLATE COURGETTE AND CARROT CAKE

Yield: 10 slices     Preparation Time: 10 minutes     Cook Time: 1 hour

## INGREDIENTS

4 medium bananas really ripe and brown

1 1/2 cup buckwheat flour

1/2 cup cocoa powder

1 tbsp bicarbonate soda

1/2 cup date syrup

1 medium courgette grated

2 medium carrots grated

1/2 cup pumpkin or sunflower seeds

1/2 cup pistachio or walnuts

Salt

## METHOD

Preheat your oven to 180 C. Line a 2lb loaf tin with baking parchment.

Process the bananas until smooth in a food processor.

Add all the other ingredients to the processor and mix thoroughly.

Transfer the mixture into the loaf tin and bake for one hour.

You might have to cover the cake with a piece of baking parchment halfway through to stop the top from cooking too much.

Remove and cool on a rack before serving.

**NOTES:** *You can freeze slices of this cake and enjoy at any time.*

# COURGETTE WRAPS

Yield: 2 wraps          Preparation Time: 10 minutes          Cook Time: 20 minutes

## INGREDIENTS

1 tbsp coconut oil

1 medium courgette grated

6 tbsp arrowroot flour

2 tbsp buckwheat flour

1/2 tsp smoked paprika

1/2 tsp cumin

1/2 tsp turmeric

Salt and black pepper

Pinch cayenne pepper

2 tbsp arrowroot mixed with

3 tbs water

1 egg beaten

## METHOD

Preheat your oven to 170 C and line a baking tray with greaseproof paper, lightly grease the paper with oil.

In a bowl squeeze out the water from the courgette and throw away the bitter juices. Gently pack the courgette into a measuring cup - you need 1 cup of courgette.

Mix the dry ingredients in a bowl.

Add the courgette and beaten egg and mix thoroughly to form a stiff batter.

Tip half the mixture onto the tray and spread as thinly as possible. Repeat with the remaining batter.

Bake for between 20 - 25 minutes, depending on the thickness. The wraps should be golden brown and still a little soft.

Fill with my recipe for Cannellini and Pepper Fajitas or your own filling.

**NOTES:** *These are wonderful with Mexican food, and they freeze really well.*

# COURGETTEE EGGS

Yield: 4 portions          Preparation Time: 10 minutes          Cook Time: 20 minutes

## INGREDIENTS

2 medium courgettes grated

2 cloves garlic crushed

1 chilli finely chopped

2/3 cup coconut flour

2 tsp turmeric

Salt and black pepper

2 eggs beaten

Coconut oil

## METHOD

Heat your oven to 200 C. Line a baking tin with baking parchment and grease with the coconut oil.

Squeeze out all of the bitter juices from the courgettes with your hands. Tip into a bowl and add the garlic, chilli, flour, turmeric, salt and black pepper stirring well. Mix in the beaten eggs.

Roll a small handful of the mixture into a ball and place on the baking tin. Repeat until all the mixture is shaped.

Bake in the oven for 20 minutes turning once. They should be golden brown. You can also fry these in a little coconut oil instead.

**NOTES:** *These balls are great served hot or cold and are lovely for a picnic.*

# 'COUSCOUS' SALAD

Yield: 4 portions          Preparation Time: 10 minutes

## INGREDIENTS

3 cups quinoa cooked

1 medium red onion finely chopped

1 red pepper finely chopped

1 small bunch fresh herbs chopped

1 lemon zest and juice

2 tbsp olive oil

1 tsp cinnamon

1 tsp cumin

1 tsp turmeric

Salt and black pepper

## METHOD

Mix everything together and check the seasoning, adjust as necessary. Leave for the flavours to infuse for a couple of hours if possible but not essential.

**NOTES:** *This dish can be used as the main part of a salad or as a side dish. It's very fresh and comforting at the same time.*

# CREAMY BEETROOT SALAD

Yield: 4 portions          Preparation Time: 10 minutes

## INGREDIENTS

3 medium beetroot cooked
1/3 cup mayonnaise
2 cloves garlic crushed
2 tbsp apple cider vinegar
Salt and black pepper

## METHOD

Roughly chop the beetroot and place in the food processor.

Add the rest of the ingredients and pulse just a few times to break up the beetroot and combine everything together.

**NOTES:** *The recipe is Russian and usually has the addition of chopped walnuts, but I personally prefer it without them. You choose.*

# CRISPS

## INGREDIENTS

2 tbsp coconut oil

1 tsp turmeric

Salt and black pepper

Herbs or seasoning of
your choice

Peelings from 4 large potatoes
(I make these when I need
peeled potatoes)

## METHOD

Preheat the oven to 200 C.

On a large baking tray add the coconut oil,
turmeric, herbs, salt and pepper. Allow to heat up
in the oven until the oil has melted.

Once heated add the potato peelings to the tray
and stir to coat the peelings.

Return to the oven and roast for 10 minutes.

Remove from the oven and stir thoroughly.

Keep repeating every 10 minutes until golden
brown.

Drain on kitchen paper and eat whilst still warm.

NOTES: *So scrummy.*

# CRISPY BEEF

Yield: 2 portions          Preparation Time: 15 minutes          Cook Time: 15 minutes

## INGREDIENTS

250g grass fed rump steak very thinly sliced

2 tbsp toasted sesame oil

1 tbsp tamari (wheat free soya sauce)

1/4 cup cornflour

1/4 cup coconut oil

1 small onion thinly sliced

1 red pepper thinly sliced

2 tsp orange zest

2 tbsp ginger grated

3 garlic cloves finely chopped

### Sauce

1/4 cup coconut sugar

1/4 cup rice wine vinegar

1/4 cup orange juice

2 tbsp tamari (wheat free soya sauce)

## METHOD

In a bowl add the beef, toasted sesame oil and tamari, mix well, then add the cornflour and again mix.

Heat the oil in a wok or pan over medium-high heat and when hot fry the beef until crispy. Remove from pan and keep warm.

Drain all but 2 tablespoons of oil from the wok. Add the onions, pepper, orange zest, ginger, and garlic to the oil and cook for 2 - 3 minutes until slightly softened. Remove from the pan and keep warm.

Meanwhile in a bowl mix the sauce ingredients - coconut sugar, vinegar, orange juice and tamari.

Add this mixture to the wok and bring to a boil. Simmer until the mixture gets thick, which takes a couple of minutes.

Return the beef and vegetables back to the pan and mix well. Warm through.

NOTES: *Serve with some fermented Kimchi and stir-fried vegetables.*

# FAJITA SPICE MIX

Yield: see notes          Preparation Time: 5 minutes

## INGREDIENTS

4 parts salt

4 parts paprika

4 parts garlic powder

4 parts onion powder

4 parts dried oregano

1 part chilli powder

1 part mustard seeds

1 part cinnamon

1 part nutmeg

## METHOD

Mix all the ingredients together, ideally in a food processor.

**NOTES:** *If one part is equal to one tablespoon the total amount made will be suitable for 12 portions. Use this spice mixture to make the easiest Fajitas you have ever made. Try my recipe for Cannellini and Pepper Fajitas.*

# FENNEL APPLE
# AND WALNUT SALAD

Yield: 4 portions          Preparation Time: 10 minutes

## INGREDIENTS

**Salad**

1 medium fennel bulb

1 apple

1/4 cup walnuts pieces

**Vinaigrette**

1/2 tsp mustard

4 tbsp apple cider vinegar

4 tbsp olive oil

Salt and black pepper
to taste

## METHOD

Very finely slice the fennel into a bowl.

Grate the apple, keeping the skin on, into the bowl and add the walnuts.

In a small glass jar add the ingredients for the vinaigrette and shake until combined.

Pour over the fennel, apple and walnuts mixing thoroughly. This will stop the apple from going brown.

If possible let the salad sit in the fridge for at least 30 minutes before serving.

**NOTES:** *This is a really refreshing salad and keeps well for a couple of days.*

# FERMENTED GARLIC CASHEW 'CHEESE'

Yield: approx 6 portions          Preparation Time: 15 minutes          Fermenting Time: up to 2 days

## INGREDIENTS

1 1/2 cups cashews, soaked overnight, rinsed and well drained

1/4 cup water

2 probiotic capsules

1 garlic clove finely crushed

1 tsp salt

3 tbsp nutritional yeast

2 tsp lemon juice

## METHOD

In a high-speed blender (you can use a blender or stick blender, but you might need to add a little more water) add the soaked cashew nuts and water. Open the probiotic capsules and tip the contents into the mixture and blend until really smooth.

Line a sieve with a nut bag and place over a bowl. Add the nut mixture, twist the nut bag so that any excess liquid just starts to form on the surface of the bag. Be gentle. You only want to gently form the nut mixture into a ball in the sieve. If you squeeze too hard, the cheese will squeeze through the mesh. Put a weight on the top (I use a jam jar filled with water), cover with a clean tea towel and leave on your work counter for no more than 48 hours to ripen. The smell will change to one that reminds you of cheese.

Tip into a bowl and add the crushed garlic, salt, nutritional yeast and lemon juice. Mix together thoroughly. Shape the cheese by using a mould and place in the fridge for a few hours to firm up.

Wash your nut bag in warm soapy water until completely clean and then sterilize. Milton Baby Fluid is an option. If you skip this process, your next batch of cheese might go mouldy. It's not worth the risk.

**NOTES:** *Nut cheeses are delicious and are actually really easy to make. It will keep for at least 1 week in the fridge, or you can freeze it in portions.*

# FERMENTED COOKED BEETROOT

Yield: varies          Preparation Time: 10 minutes          Fermenting Time: 4 days

## INGREDIENTS

3 large beetroot cooked

3 tbsp salt

3 cups water

2 cups apple cider vinegar

## METHOD

Dissolve the salt in the water. I use a mason jar which can be used for the fermenting.

Chop up the beetroot into 1/2" cubes.

Add to the brine, ensuring the beetroot is submerged.

Cover and leave to ferment on your work counter for 2 days.

Drain off the brine (you can drink the liquid - having a small shot glass per day) and top up the jar with the apple cider vinegar. You might not need to use it all, just ensure all the beetroot is submerged. Allow the beetroot to ferment in the vinegar for a further 2 days and then store in the fridge.

NOTES: *This is lovely served whenever you have a salad. It tastes very similar to the beetroot in vinegar you can buy, but you are getting a double fermented product. So much healthier than the malt vinegar version.*

# FERMENTED CRUSTED ALMOND 'CHEESE'

Yield: 8 portions          Preparation Time: 15 minutes          Fermenting Time: up to 2 days

## INGREDIENTS

2 cups almonds soaked overnight

1 cup water

1 tsp brown miso (optional)

3 probiotic capsules

3 tbsp nutritional yeast

Pinch nutmeg

Salt and black pepper

## METHOD

Gently squeeze each almond to remove the skins. Rinse thoroughly under running water. This helps to remove some of the enzyme inhibitors, so you gain more nutrients from the nuts.

In a high-speed blender add the soaked skinned almonds, water and brown miso. Open the probiotic capsules and tip the contents into the mixture. Blend until really smooth.

Line a sieve with a nut bag and place over a bowl.

Add the nut mixture, twist the nut bag so that any excess liquid just starts to form on the surface of the bag. Be gentle. You only want to gently form the nut mixture into a ball in the sieve. If you squeeze too hard, the cheese will squeeze through the mesh. Put a weight on the top (I use a jam jar filled with water), cover with a clean tea towel and leave on your work counter for no more than 48 hours to ripen. The smell will change to one that reminds you of cheese.

Tip into a bowl and add the nutritional yeast, nutmeg and mix together. If you are going to coat the cheese with salt and pepper, then don't add any extra salt. If you aren't going to coat the cheese, then add salt to taste.

*more -*

NOTES: *The 'cheese' will keep for at least 1 week in the fridge, or you can freeze it in portions.*

# FERMENTED CRUSTED ALMOND 'CHEESE'

## METHOD CONTINUED

Press into a mould. Refrigerate for about 4 hours to firm up. Gently ease out of the mould.

Coat the cheese with the crushed black pepper and salt.

Place in a dehydrator for 8 hours at 40 C or 110 F to firm up the outside which forms a crust. You can skip this step if you don't have a dehydrator.

Wash your nut bag in warm soapy water until completely clean and then sterilize. Milton Baby Fluid is an option. If you skip this process, your next batch of cheese might go mouldy. Trust me it's not worth the risk.

# FERMENTED CUCUMBER

Yield: 8 portions     Preparation Time: 10 minutes     Fermenting Time: 2-3 days

## INGREDIENTS

1 cucumber chopped into 1/2" pieces

1 tbsp salt

1 tbsp ginger grated

1 large clove garlic crushed

1 tsp Gochugaru – see Notes (or a pinch of cayenne pepper)

1 tbsp apple cider vinegar

## METHOD

Sprinkle the cucumber with the salt and leave covered for a couple of hours. The salt will draw out the water from the cucumber.

Mix the remaining ingredients into the cucumber and water mixture.

Press down into a mason jar ensuring the cucumber is submerged in the brine liquid. Close your jar.

Leave to ferment for 2 or 3 days on your work counter until the cucumber turns translucent. Stir every day.

Store in the fridge and eat within 3 weeks.

**NOTES:** *You can make this with normal chilli powder, but it really is worth the trouble of sourcing the Gochugaru which can be purchased from an online company called Sous Chef. This is great served in place of pickled gherkins or chopped into salads.*

# FERMENTED
# FIG CHUTNEY

Yield: 12 portions          Preparation Time: 10 minutes          Fermenting Time: 5 days

## INGREDIENTS

1 1/2 cups raisins soaked in boiling water 20 minutes

1/2 cup water from the soaked raisins

1/4 tsp mixed spice

2 tsp salt

2 cloves garlic

3 probiotic capsules

12 small fresh figs

1 small red onion chopped

## METHOD

Drain the raisins and squeeze out the excess water, reserving 1/2 cup of the water. Add to your food processor together with the rest of the ingredients, except the figs and onion. Process until smooth.

Cut off the top of the figs and quarter them. Add to a bowl followed by the red onion and raisin mixture. Mix gently, trying not to break up the fig quarters. Pack into a mason jar and ensure there are no air pockets.

Leave to ferment for about 5 days on your kitchen counter. Open the jar each day to release any pressure.

Once you are happy with the flavour store in the fridge for up to 4 weeks.

NOTES: *This is delightful served with any of the nut cheeses for a snack or lunch.*

# FERMENTED KIMCHI

Yield: approx 20 portions     Preparation Time: 15 minutes     Fermenting Time: 7 days

## INGREDIENTS

3 tbsp salt

3 cups water

1 outside cabbage leaf

1 white cabbage sliced or chopped

1 cup onion chopped

1 red pepper sliced

1 carrot thinly sliced

1 cup of sprouted mung beans

2 cloves garlic chopped

2 tbsp ginger grated

4 tsp Gochugaru – see Notes (or 1/4 tsp cayenne pepper)

## METHOD

In a jug dissolve the salt in one cup of hot water and when dissolved add the extra two cups of cold water.

In a large bowl add all the ingredients except the outer leaf and mix thoroughly. Pack the vegetable mixture into a large mason jar and use either your fist or the end of a rolling pin to push and squash the vegetables together. Everything needs to be as condensed as possible.

Tip the brine solution gently into the mason jar and let it settle. The water will seep between the pieces of vegetables. It's the brine solution that stops the vegetables from going mouldy.

The outer cabbage leaf is used to hold the vegetables under the brine. Close the lid and leave on your work counter for around 7 days to ferment.

Open the jar each day to release any pressure. At the end of a week drain off the excess liquid, remove the cabbage leaf and store in the fridge for a couple of months.

**NOTES:** *You can make this with normal chilli powder, but it really is worth the trouble of sourcing the Gochugaru which can be purchased from an online company called Sous Chef.*

*This goes really well with Thai and Chinese food.*

# FERMENTED KOMBUCHA

Yield: approx 3/4 litre          Preparation Time: 10 minutes          Fermenting Time: 7 - 21 days

## INGREDIENTS

1/3 cup of unrefined sugar

3 scoops loose leaf black or green tea (it needs to contain caffeine)

3/4 litre of water

1 SCOBY (I bought mine from eBay)

## METHOD

Boil about 1/2 of the water and add half (1/4 overall water) to the sugar in a one-litre mason jar. Stir to dissolve. Make the tea with the remaining boiling the water (1/4 overall water) and leave to brew for approximately 20 minutes.

Strain the tea, add to the sugar water and top up with the remaining cold water. Test the temperature of the water - it should be no hotter than tepid. Gently put the SCOBY on top and cover the opening of the jar with some kitchen paper and a rubber band. It needs to breathe.

Place somewhere warm and dark. An airing cupboard is ideal. Leave for about 7 days. If the temperature is too cold, the process will take longer. Taste as you go along, the longer you leave it, the less sweet it becomes. The SCOBY may sink but don't worry, a new "baby" will form a seal on the top of the liquid. After it has brewed, remove the SCOBY (original and the "baby") and a little of the Kombucha and set to one side so that you can start the process again.

Strain the amber liquid into a bottle with a screw top or one of the old-fashioned lemonade bottles. Leave the finished Kombucha out of the fridge for a few days, and it may go fizzy, then store in the fridge. Each time it will taste different.

**NOTES:** *The SCOBY will die if it comes into contact with metal, so use plastic or wooden utensils only.*

# FERMENTED LIMES

Yield: 500ml mason jar          Preparation Time: 10 minutes          Fermenting Time: 5 days

## INGREDIENTS

8 limes cut into quarters
4 tbsp of salt

## METHOD

Add your limes and salt into a food processor and pulse together until the size of breadcrumbs then transfer to the glass mason jar. Press down to ensure all the air pockets are removed; this is the important part. It's the air that can cause the limes to go mouldy.

Leave to ferment for about 5 or so days until the rind of the limes turns translucent.

Store in the fridge for up to 6 months.

**NOTES:** *I love to have these with any Indian food or alternatively sprinkled over a salad. Try adding some Indian spices to the mix in the food processor.*

# FERMENTED VEGETABLES

Yield: 1500ml mason jar          Preparation Time: 15 minutes          Fermenting Time: 7 days

## INGREDIENTS

1 outer leaf of the cabbage

Cabbage stalk

1 medium cabbage

1 medium onion

3 medium carrots

3 tbsp salt

## METHOD

I use a food processor to chop all the vegetables except the outer leaf and stalk of the cabbage. The size of a sweetcorn is ideal.

In a large bowl add all the vegetables and salt mixing thoroughly. Leave covered on your work counter for a few hours and occasionally mix with a spoon. The juices from the vegetables should start to come out, and the mixture will become wet.

Press the vegetable mixture into the large glass mason jar and pack down firmly. The aim is to eliminate all the air. Ideally, you want a couple of inches gap at the top of the jar. The water released from the vegetables should rise up over the cabbage mixture. Use the cabbage leaf to hold the vegetables under the brine and if necessary use part of the cabbage stalk to help with this. When you close the lid, the liquid should completely cover your vegetable mixture.

Place the mason jar in a bowl in case of any leaking. The contents will expand. Leave on your work counter for about 7 days to ferment. Each day open the jar to release the pressure and seal again. I call this burping. You might have to tip a little of the excess brine away because more will be created from the mixture.

At the end of a week remove and throw away the cabbage leaf and stalk and drain off the excess liquid. It will keep in the fridge for months.

NOTES: *Try and have a tablespoon a day to keep the bacteria balanced in your gut.*

# FERMENTED WATER KEFIR

Yield: approx 3/4 litre          Preparation Time: 15 minutes          Fermenting Time: 2 - 7 days

## INGREDIENTS

1/3 cup of unrefined sugar

1/3 cup of Kefir grains (I bought mine originally from eBay)

3/4 litre of water

## METHOD

Boil about 1/4 of your water. Add the sugar and boiling water into a one-litre jar with a metal spoon in it to stop the jar from cracking. Once dissolved top up with the remaining cold water. Test the temperature of the water - it should be no hotter than tepid. Remove the metal spoon. The Kefir grains can be killed by metal.

Gently tip the Kefir grains in, and they will sink to the bottom. Cover with a piece of kitchen paper and an elastic band. It needs to breathe.

Place somewhere warm and dark - an airing cupboard is ideal, for about 48 hours. If the temperature is too cold, the process will take longer. Taste as you go along, the longer you leave it, the less sweet it becomes.

Once you are happy with the taste, sieve the liquid through a non-metal sieve into a screw top bottle or one of the old-fashioned lemonade bottles. Keep a little of the liquid and the grains to one side so that you can start the process again.

At this point, you can add the juice from 1/2 a lemon or some grated ginger to change the flavour.

Leave the finished Kefir out of the fridge for a few days, and it may go fizzy. Then store in the fridge.

NOTES: *The grains grow with each batch made, so you can either increase the amount you make each time or give some of the Kefir grains to a friend.*

# JULOAF

Yield: 6 portions         Preparation Time: 20 minutes         Cook Time: 40 minutes

## INGREDIENTS

2 tbsp coconut oil

1 large onion chopped

3 cloves garlic crushed

1 chilli chopped

1 large carrot grated

1/4 cup raisins

1 1/2 cups Puy lentils cooked

2 cups quinoa cooked

1 tsp fennel seeds coarsely ground

3 tbsp flax meal

1 tsp mixed herbs

1 tsp turmeric

2 tbsp vegan Worcestershire sauce

3 tbsp tomato paste

3 tbsp nutritional yeast

1/2 cup buckwheat flour

Salt and black pepper

## METHOD

Preheat your oven to 180 C. Line a 2 lb loaf tin with a parchment liner.

Heat the oil in a pan over a medium heat and gently fry the onions, garlic and chilli for 5 minutes or until translucent. If you cover the pan and add a pinch of salt it encourages the onions to soften. Stir occasionally.

Add the carrots, raisins and spices. Cover and gently cook for another 5 minutes, stirring occasionally.

Remove from the heat and add the rest of the ingredients. Use a potato masher and really mash together. Taste and add more seasoning if required. The mixture should resemble a burger patty. Press the mixture very firmly into the lined tin and bake for 30 minutes.

Allow to rest for 15 minutes before slicing.

NOTES: *This is just as nice served cold with salad as well as in place of meat with a roast dinner.*

# LENTIL SPINACH AND RED PEPPER CURRY

Yield: 4 portions      Preparation Time: 10 minutes      Cook Time: 50 minutes

## INGREDIENTS

2 cups Puy lentils (ideally soaked 16 hours)

3 tbsp coconut oil

2 large onions chopped

6 garlic cloves crushed

1" ginger grated

4 tbsp curry powder

1 red pepper finely sliced

1 can coconut milk full fat

2 cups stock

5 or so handfuls of spinach

Salt and black pepper

## METHOD

Soak your lentils for 16 hours if possible to help remove the phytic acid, but if you don't have time you can skip this step. Rinse your lentils thoroughly under running water and set to one side to drain the excess liquid.

Heat the oil and gently fry the onions, garlic and ginger for 5 minutes until golden brown, stirring occasionally. Add the curry powder and stir for a couple of minutes.

Add the lentils together with the coconut milk and stock. Cover and simmer very gently for 30 minutes. Stir occasionally.

Season with the salt and black pepper to taste then add the sliced red pepper, replace the lid and simmer for a further 5 minutes.

Add the spinach and mix into the lentil mixture. Allow to wilt for a minute.

**NOTES:** *Serve with some cauliflower rice and my Carrot Ginger and Cardamom salad. It freezes exceptionally well.*

# MUSHROOM STROGANOFF

Yield: 2 portions          Preparation Time: 10 minutes          Cook Time: 15 minutes

## INGREDIENTS

2 cups rice pasta uncooked

Salt

1 tbsp coconut oil

1 large garlic clove crushed

1 medium onion sliced

2 cups mushrooms chopped

1/2 tsp mixed herbs

1/4 whole nutmeg grated

3/4 cup of cashew nuts soaked overnight

1 1/2 cups water

1 tsp mustard

1 tbsp balsamic vinegar

Salt and black pepper

## METHOD

Cook the pasta in plenty of boiling water with salt according to the packet and drain once cooked. Keep warm if possible, but it's not essential.

Gently fry the onion, garlic, herbs and nutmeg for 5 minutes, stirring occasionally. A pinch of salt and a lid speeds up the process.

In a blender add the soaked cashew nuts, water, mustard and balsamic vinegar blending until silky smooth.

Add the mushrooms to the onions and cook for a couple of minutes until just beginning to wilt. Add the drained pasta.

Pour in the 'cream' which you have made with the cashew nuts and allow to heat through.

The sauce will start to be absorbed by the pasta and thicken slightly.

**NOTES:** *Serve with my Fennel Apple and Walnut Salad together with Creamy Beetroot Salad.*

# ONION FRITTERS

Yield: 4 portions        Preparation Time: 10 minutes        Cook Time: 10 minutes

## INGREDIENTS

1 medium onion finely sliced

1/4 cup fresh herbs chopped

1 tsp turmeric

Salt and black pepper

1/2 cup gram flour (chickpea)

3 tbsp water

3 tbsp coconut oil

## METHOD

Mix the onions with the herbs, turmeric, salt and black pepper.

Sieve the flour into the onion mixture and mix thoroughly.

Add the water and mix to form a slight batter. You might need to add a little more water but be careful not to add too much.

Shallow fry in coconut oil on a medium heat for about 5 minutes each side, until golden brown.

**NOTES:** *These are a wonderful alternative to traditional onion rings. They also freeze exceptionally well and can be reheated in an oven at 180 C for about 20 minutes from frozen.*

# 'PASTA' CARBONARA WITH PARMESAN 'CHEESE'

Yield: 2 portions          Preparation Time: 15 minutes          Cook Time: 15 minutes

## INGREDIENTS

**Parmesan 'Cheese'**

4 tbsp nutritional yeast

1/4 cup cashew nuts

1 tsp turmeric

1/2 tsp salt

**Main Ingredients**

2 tbsp coconut oil

1 medium onion finely sliced

2 cloves garlic crushed

1 red pepper finely sliced

8 chestnut mushrooms finely sliced

2 medium courgettes

**Sauce**

1 cup of cashew nuts soaked overnight

3/4 cup water

6 tbsp nutritional yeast

Salt and black pepper

## METHOD

In a food processor pulse the parmesan cheese ingredients together. Tip into a bowl.

Gently fry the onions and garlic for 5 minutes, covering with a lid. Add the peppers and mushrooms, stir and cover on a low heat for about 5 minutes until slightly softened.

In a blender add all the sauce ingredients and process until silky smooth.

If you have a Spirilizer, then turn the courgettes into 'spaghetti'. If not then use a vegetable peeler and make very thin strips.

When the onions, peppers and mushrooms are cooked, add the sauce, courgettes and stir until well combined. The courgettes should only wilt a little.

Serve the Carbonara in bowls and sprinkle with the 'cheese'.

**NOTES:** *Add a big bowl of salad and fermented vegetables. Real comfort food.*

# RAW CARROT AND CITRUS CAKE

Yield: 6 - 8 portions    Preparation Time: 20 minutes    Chill Time: 2 hours

## INGREDIENTS

**Cake**
1/2 cup currants soaked in water for 2 hours
2 large carrots chopped
1 cup walnuts plus 8 to garnish
1/4 cup desiccated coconut
1/3 cup coconut oil melted
1/4 cup maple syrup
2 tsp cinnamon
1/2 tsp nutmeg

**Frosting**
1/2 block coconut cream (100g)
1 cup cashews soaked overnight
1/4 cup water
1 lemon zest and juice
1 tbsp vanilla extract
3 tbsp raw maple syrup
2 or 3 tbsp almond milk

## METHOD

Line the bottom of an 8" spring cake tin. Drain the currants and gently squeeze out the water. Process with the carrots in a food processor until like fine breadcrumbs. Add the rest of the cake ingredients and pulse. Do not over process. Tip the mixture into the lined tin and press down firmly. Pop in the freezer while you make the frosting.

To make the frosting melt the half block of coconut cream in a bowl over a pan of simmering water (Bain Marie).

Process the cashew nuts and water in a blender until silky smooth. When the coconut cream has melted, add the lemon zest, juice, vanilla extract, maple syrup and the silky cashew nuts. Mix thoroughly.

Top the cake with the frosting. If you like you could layer the cake and coat completely with the frosting, depending on how much time you have.

Refrigerate for a couple of hours to firm up.

**NOTES:** *This cake is yummy. The frosting can even be piped onto individual portion-sized cakes to look just like cupcakes. It can be frozen as well.*

# RAW CHOCOLATE
# AND ALMOND TRUFFLES

Yield: 30 chocolates          Preparation Time: 10 minutes          Freezer Timer: 1 hour

## INGREDIENTS

1/2 cup coconut oil
5 tbsp almond butter
7 tbsp raw cacao
3 tbsp date syrup
1 tsp vanilla extract
Salt
Raw cacao for dusting

## METHOD

Gently melt the coconut oil in a bowl over a pan of simmering water (Bain Marie). Whisk in the other ingredients. Pour into individual chocolate moulds and pop into your freezer for at least an hour. When you have removed them from the moulds, you can dust with the raw cacao powder.

**NOTES:** *I'm always amazed that something so decadent can actually be good for you.*

# RAW CHOCOLATE AND ORANGE CAKE

Yield: 6 - 8 portions          Preparation Time: 15 minutes          Chill Time: 2 hours

## INGREDIENTS

**Base/Frosting**
1 block coconut cream (200g)
1/3 cup coconut oil
1 tbsp vanilla extract
1/3 cup maple or date syrup
1/4 cup raw cacao
1 tbsp orange extract
Salt

**Cake**
1 cup sultanas soaked in green tea for 2 hours
1 medium sweet potato chopped
1 cup walnuts pieces
1/4 cup raw cacao
1/2 orange zest and juice
1 tbsp orange extract

## METHOD

Line the base of an 8" spring cake tin with baking parchment.

Melt the block of coconut cream and coconut oil in a bowl over a pan of simmering water (Bain Marie).

Strain the sultanas removing as much tea as possible. Process with the sweet potato in a food processor until like breadcrumbs.

Add the walnuts, cacao powder, orange zest, juice and orange extract and pulse a few times to mix thoroughly.

By now the coconut cream and oil should have melted. Add the rest of the base/frosting ingredients and use a whisk to mix thoroughly.

Add half of the melted coconut and chocolate mixture to the sweet potato and mix thoroughly. The remaining half is your frosting.

Tip into your cake tin and press firmly down.

Pour over the remaining base/frosting mixture and refrigerate for a couple of hours to firm up.

**NOTES:** *The cake will keep in the fridge for 3 days, or you can slice and freeze in individual slices.*

# RAW CHOCOLATE
# AND PEPPERMINT SLICE

Yield: 20 slices          Preparation Time: 30 minutes          Chill Time: 2 hours

## INGREDIENTS

**Base**
3/4 cup apricots chopped soaked 20 minutes
1/3 cup dates chopped soaked 20 minutes
1 1/2 cups desiccated coconut
1/3 cup raw cacao

**Filling**
1 cup cashews soaked overnight
2 cups desiccated coconut
3/4 cup coconut oil
1/2 cup maple syrup
1/2 tsp vanilla extract
5 tsp peppermint extract

**Topping**
1/2 cup coconut oil
1/2 cup raw cacao
3 tbsp maple syrup
1 tbsp vanilla extract
Pinch salt

## METHOD

Line an 8" baking tin with greaseproof paper.

Drain the fruit, squeezing out the excess water, then process in a food processor with the coconut and cacao powder until everything is well mixed.

Tip the mixture into the tin and make an even layer. I use damp hands.

Process all the filling ingredients until really smooth and then spread on top of the base.

To make the topping melt the coconut oil in a bowl over a pan of boiling water (Bain Marie). Add the rest of the topping ingredients and whisk. Pour over the top of the cream filling and place in the fridge for a couple of hours or the freezer if you're in a hurry. Lift out and slice as needed.

NOTES: *This reminds me of Fry's Chocolate Cream. You can freeze individual slices.*

# RAW CHOCOLATE AND WALNUT BROWNIES

Yield: 9 portions       Preparation Time: 15 minutes       Chill Time: 2 hours

## INGREDIENTS

### Frosting

3 tbsp coconut oil

1/4 cup raw cacao

3 tbsp sweetener such as maple or date syrup

2 tsp pure vanilla extract

Salt

### Brownie

2 cups dates chopped

1 cups walnut pieces plus a few to garnish

1/4 cup raw cacao

2 tsp pure vanilla extract

1 tbsp water

Salt

## METHOD

Line an 8" square container with parchment paper.

For the frosting, melt the coconut oil In a medium mixing bowl over a pan of simmering water (Bain Marie). Turn off the heat and remove the bowl from the pan. Keep to one side.

Add all the brownie ingredients into your food processor and process until completely smooth, scraping down the bowl as needed - don't be tempted to add any extra water.

Transfer the dough to your container and press very firmly until evenly distributed. Damp hands work well.

Add the rest of the frosting ingredients to the melted coconut oil and whisk. Then pour over your dough.

Garnish with the extra walnuts.

Pop into the fridge for a couple of hours then cut into portions.

NOTES: *Store in the fridge for up to 2 weeks or in your freezer.*

# RAW CHOCOLATE CARAMEL AND VANILLA ICE CREAM

Yield: 8 portions     Preparation Time: 30 minutes     Freezer Time: 4 hours

## INGREDIENTS

**Chocolate Layer**
4 tbsp coconut oil
3 tbsp maple syrup
4 tbsp raw cacao

**Caramel**
2 tbsp coconut oil
8 Medjool dates pitted
1 tbsp maple syrup
1 tsp vanilla extract
Salt

**Ice Cream**
1 cup cashews soaked overnight
1/2 block coconut cream (100g)
1/4 cup maple syrup
1/4 cup almond milk
2 tsp vanilla extract
Salt

## METHOD

To make the chocolate layer, melt the coconut oil in a bowl over a pan of boiling water (Bain Marie) very gently. Whisk in the cacao and when smooth add the maple syrup, vanilla and salt.

Pour into a silicone cupcake mould and pop into the freezer while you make the caramel.

Next, make the caramel by processing the ingredients in a blender until smooth. You will have to stop and scrape down the date mixture a few times. Divide equally onto the chocolate layer. Pop back into the freezer while you make the ice cream.

Drain and rinse the cashew nuts. Add all the ice cream ingredients into your blender and mix until silky smooth. Add a little more almond milk if too thick. Divide equally over the caramel mixture and freeze for a minimum of 2 hours.

Remove from the freezer for 5 minutes before serving.

NOTES: *These keep beautifully for a month in the freezer.*

# RAW CHOCOLATE ICE CREAM

Yield: 2 portions     Preparation Time: 5 minutes     Freezer Time: 2 hours

## INGREDIENTS

1 large avocado

1/4 cup coconut yoghurt (you can use any)

1/2 cup almond milk

1/4 cup raw cacao

3 tbsp date syrup

1 tbsp vanilla extract

Pinch salt

## METHOD

Process all the ingredients until really smooth. Check for sweetness.

Pour into a dish and freeze for 1 hour, remove and use a fork to break up the frozen pieces and remix. Return to the freezer and repeat again after an hour. You can then serve it or keep in the freezer until needed.

Allow to soften up for a few minutes before you eat.

NOTES: *You can freeze in lolly moulds if you prefer.*

# RAW COCONUT
# AND APRICOT BALLS

Yield: 30 balls          Preparation Time: 15 minutes          Chill Time: 1 hour

## INGREDIENTS

3/4 cup apricots chopped
soaked for 20 mins

1/3 cup dates chopped
soaked for 20 mins

1 1/2 cups desiccated coconut

1/3 cup raw cacao

Pinch salt

Dusting of raw cacao to
decorate

## METHOD

Drain the fruit, squeezing out the excess
water, then process in a food processor with
the coconut, cacao powder and salt until
everything is fairly smooth.

Dampen your hands and take out a teaspoon
size amount and roll in damp hands until it
forms a small ball. Repeat the process until
the mixture is used up.

Lightly dust with raw cacao.

These are best eaten after they have been in
the fridge for about an hour if you can wait
that long.

**NOTES:** *The balls can be frozen and taken out as needed. If they are refrigerated
they will keep for a week.*

# RAW HUMMUS

Yield: 4 portions          Preparation Time: 10 minutes          Chill Time: 30 minutes

## INGREDIENTS

2 medium courgettes
1/2 cup tahini
1 small garlic clove crushed
1 tsp cumin
1 small lemon zest and juice
Salt
3 tbsp extra virgin olive oil
Extra virgin olive oil to drizzle
Pinch cayenne pepper

## METHOD

Peel your courgettes unless you'd like a green hummus. Grate coarsely. Using your hands squeeze out the bitter juices. You need about 2 cups of the loosely packed grated courgettes. Place into your food processor.

Add the tahini, garlic, cumin, lemon zest and juice together with the olive oil and process until smooth. You might like to add some more lemon juice and seasoning to taste.

Leave for half an hour or so for the flavours to mingle in the fridge.

Serve on a deep plate or bowl drizzled with some olive oil and a pinch of cayenne pepper.

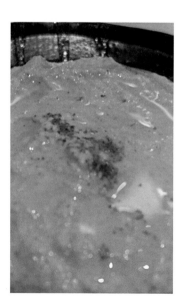

**NOTES:** *This hummus is now my favourite and is so much easier to make than the traditional version using chickpeas. Much healthier too.*

# RAW KIWI AND AVOCADO LOLLIES

Yield: 4 lollies          Preparation Time: 10 minutes          Freezer Time: 4 hours

## INGREDIENTS

3 kiwi fruits peeled
1 large avocado
3 tbsp maple syrup
1 lemon zest
1/2 lemon squeezed

## METHOD

In a blender process all the ingredients until smooth. I don't like things too sweet so taste and add more maple syrup and/or lemon according to taste.

Pour into your lolly moulds and freeze for a few hours.

NOTES: *Why would you want to buy a normal lolly? These are refreshing and creamy at the same time.*

# RAW LAYERED CHOCOLATE DELIGHTS

Yield: 12     Preparation Time: 20 minutes     Freezer Time: 20 minutes

## INGREDIENTS

1/4 block coconut cream (50g)

1/4 cup coconut oil

1/4 cup raw cacao

3 tbsp maple syrup

2 tsp vanilla extract

2 tbsp goji berries and nuts finely chopped

## METHOD

Double up 12 petit four cases on a freezer-proof tray.

Melt the coconut cream in a bowl over simmering water (Bain Marie) and pour a teaspoon into each petit four case. Place them in the freezer for about 10 minutes.

To make the chocolate layer, melt the coconut oil in a bowl over simmering water (Bain Marie). Add the raw cacao and mix thoroughly. Whisk in the maple syrup and vanilla extract.

Remove the cases from the freezer and pour the chocolate layer over the coconut cream.

Sprinkle with the finely chopped goji berries and nuts and freeze for another 10 minutes.

**NOTES:** *You can vary the toppings or even add nuts or dried fruit between the layers. Try adding a couple of tablespoons of Maca or Lucuma powder for a twist.*

# RAW MARINATED MUSHROOMS

Yield: 2 portions          Preparation Time: 5 minutes          Rest Time: 30 minutes

## INGREDIENTS

3 tbsp olive oil

1/2 lemon zest and juice

1 tbsp tamari (wheat free soya sauce)

Pinch cayenne pepper (optional)

1/2 tsp turmeric

Salt and black pepper

1 handful chopped herbs

1 small punnet chestnut mushrooms

## METHOD

Mix all the ingredients in a bowl except for the mushrooms.

Slice the mushrooms then add to the bowl. Mix thoroughly to coat the mushrooms.

Leave to marinate for 30 minutes if possible at room temperature or for a few hours in the fridge.

If you have a dehydrator, you can pop them in at 40 C or 110 F for 4 hours.

NOTES: *If you like garlic add a crushed clove - delicious.*

# RAW 'MILK' CHOCOLATE CAKE

Yield: 6 portions          Preparation Time: 20 minutes          Chill Time: 2 hours

## INGREDIENTS

### Cake
1/2 block coconut cream (100g)
2 medium parsnips chopped
1 cup dates chopped
1 cup walnut pieces chopped
1/4 cup of raw cacao
6 tbsp maple or date syrup
3 tsp vanilla extract
Salt

### Frosting
1/2 block coconut cream (100g)
1 cup cashew nuts soaked overnight
1 tbsp vanilla extract
1/3 cup maple or date syrup
2 tbsp raw cacao
You might need 2 tbsp almond milk(optional)

## METHOD

Line the base of an 8" spring cake tin with baking parchment.

Melt the 2 half blocks of coconut cream which you'll be using in both the cake and frosting. Place in a bowl over a pan of simmering water (Bain Marie).

Process the parsnips and the dates in a food processor until like breadcrumbs. The mixture should hold together if you pinch a little between your fingers.

Add the walnuts, cacao, maple or date syrup, vanilla extract and a pinch of salt into parsnip and date mixture and pulse a few times. Add half of the melted coconut cream and pulse again to mix everything together.

Tip into your cake tin and press firmly down. Pop into the freezer for 15 minutes to set the cake. Make the frosting by adding all the frosting ingredients including the remaining half block of melted coconut cream into a high-speed blender and process until silky smooth. You may need to add a couple of tablespoons of almond milk to loosen everything up, but avoid adding if at all possible.

Remove the cake from the freezer and top with the frosting. Refrigerate for two hours before serving.

NOTES: *If you like, you could pipe the frosting onto the cake. The cake freezes really well cut into individual portions.*

# RAW
# NUT BURGERS

Yield: 4 portions          Preparation Time: 10 minutes

## INGREDIENTS

1/2 cup walnut pieces
1/2 cup almonds
1 large carrot chopped
1/2 small red onion chopped
Handful of fresh herbs
1 lemon juiced
2 tbsp ground flaxseeds
1/4 tsp turmeric
Salt and black pepper to taste (optional)

## METHOD

Add all the ingredients into a food processor being careful not to over process. You want to keep a little texture.

Taste and adjust the seasoning. Form into 8 equal patties using damp hands.

You can either eat them as they are or if you have a dehydrator you can crisp them for about 5 hours at 40 C or 110 F, although this isn't necessary. Alternatively fry them in coconut oil.

NOTES: *Don't be fooled by how easy these are. They're deliciously healthy.*

# RAW SMASHED CHICKPEA AND SWEETCORN

Yield: 4 servings          Preparation Time: 20 minutes

## INGREDIENTS

**Sauce**

1 cup cashews soaked overnight

3/4 cup water

1 tbsp apple cider vinegar

2 tsp lemon juice

**Filling**

2 cups sprouted chickpeas (see Notes)

1 cup sweetcorn

1 small red onion finely diced

1/4 small cucumber finely diced

2 stalks celery finely diced

Pinch cayenne pepper

Small handful coriander chopped

Salt and black pepper

## METHOD

Drain the cashew nuts and rinse. Add all the sauce ingredients into a high-speed blender and process until silky smooth.

In a bowl lightly crush the chickpeas with either a fork or potato masher.

Mix all the other ingredients together in a bowl, check for seasoning and serve.

**NOTES:** *My favourite way to make this is with sprouted chickpeas, but you can use cooked ones instead.*

1

# RHUBARB AND COCONUT CAKE

Yield: 10 slices        Preparation Time: 10 minutes        Cook Time: 50 minutes

## INGREDIENTS

2 cups desiccated coconut

1/2 cup buckwheat flour

2 tsp baking powder

Salt

1 cup almond milk

3 eggs beaten

1/2 cup date syrup

1 1/2 cups of finely sliced rhubarb

## METHOD

Preheat oven to 180 C. Line a 2lb loaf tin with a loaf liner or baking parchment if you don't have one.

In a food processor combine all the ingredients keeping back 1/2 of the rhubarb (3/4 cup). Pour into the loaf tin. The remaining rhubarb (raw) should be placed on top of the cake evenly and then drizzle an extra little date syrup over the top.

Bake for 50 minutes. Check after 40 minutes and if necessary cover with baking paper to stop it from burning.

Cool on a rack.

NOTES: *Yum, yum, yum. The easiest quickest cake ever and you can freeze slices individually.*

# ROASTED VEGETABLES AND QUINOA MUFFINS

Yield: 4 for lunch          Preparation Time: 15 minutes          Cook Time: 20 minutes

## INGREDIENTS

2 cups quinoa cooked

1 cup mixed roasted vegetables

2 tbsp ground flax meal

1/2 cup oats

2 tbsp tomato puree

2 tbsp tamari sauce (wheat free soya sauce)

2 tbsp nutritional yeast

Salt and black pepper

## METHOD

Preheat the oven to 180 C. Prepare your muffin tin by either greasing or using cupcake liners.

In a blender or food processor add the oats and pulse until it resembles flour.

Add all the other ingredients into a bowl together with the oat flour and mix together thoroughly, using a potato masher. Divide the mixture into the muffin tin and bake for 20 minutes.

Serve warm or cold.

NOTES: *These work really well for a packed lunch instead of sandwiches.*

# SOUP CREAMY WATERCRESS

Yield: 4 portions    Preparation Time: 10 minutes    Cook Time: 30 minutes

## INGREDIENTS

2 tbsp coconut oil

1 large onion chopped

2 garlic cloves crushed

100g watercress

1 can cannellini beans drained

3 cups vegetable stock

1 lemon zest and juice

Salt and black pepper

## METHOD

Gently heat the oil and add the chopped onion and garlic. Cut the stalks of the watercress finely and reserve the leaves for later. Add the stalks to the onions and garlic. Cover and very gently soften for about 20 minutes. Do not let it colour or burn so keep stirring every few minutes.

Add the cooked cannellini beans, watercress leaves (keep a few back to garnish), vegetable stock, lemon zest and half of the lemon juice. Bring to the boil and simmer gently for 10 minutes until the beans are soft.

Remove from the heat and blend until smooth using a stick blender. Taste and if necessary add salt, black pepper and the rest of the lemon juice. Garnish with the remaining watercress leaves.

**NOTES:** *You can substitute the watercress for young nettles for a change. Just don't get stung.*

# SOUP
# MINESTRONE

Yield: 6 portions          Preparation Time: 10 minutes          Cook Time: 20 minutes

## INGREDIENTS

2 tbsp coconut oil
1 small leek sliced
2 medium carrots thinly sliced
2 stalks celery chopped
3 garlic cloves crushed
2 tsp Herbs de Provence
1/3 cup tomato paste
4 cups vegetable stock
1 courgette chopped
2 cups Savoy cabbage finely sliced
1 cup cooked spaghetti (or Konjac noodles)
Salt and black pepper
Olive oil for serving

## METHOD

Gently heat the oil then add the chopped leek, carrot, celery, garlic and herbs. Cover and cook for 10 minutes, stirring frequently.

Stir the tomato paste into the vegetables together with the Savoy cabbage. Add the stock. Bring to the boil and gently simmer for 10 minutes. Finally, add the cooked spaghetti or Konjac noodles and warm through.

Add salt and black pepper to taste.

Serve with some olive oil swirled into the soup.

**NOTES:** *If you're using spaghetti, try and use a wheat or gluten-free variety. Alternatively, add some cooked white beans for a higher protein count.*

# SUPERFOOD SALAD

Yield: 2 portions          Preparation Time: 10 minutes

## INGREDIENTS

**Salad**
5 or 6 kale leaves
2 tbsp olive oil
Salt
1/2 pomegranate
Sprouted seeds
1 small red onion very finely sliced
2 tomatoes chopped
1 avocado chopped
2 tbsp fermented vegetables
1 tbsp fermented lemons

**Dressing**
1 clove garlic crushed
Salt
2 tbsp apple cider vinegar
4 tbsp olive oil

## METHOD

Mix the 2 tablespoons of olive oil and salt into the kale and leave for 10 minutes to wilt and soften. Remove the seeds from the pomegranate and add to the rest of the salad ingredients in a bowl.

In a pestle and mortar crush the garlic with the salt, add the vinegar and oil. Mix. Pour over the salad and serve. Alternatively just drizzle a little of the oil and vinegar on the salad.

**NOTES:** *Substitute the kale for any green leaves if you can't find it. My favourites are watercress, rocket and spinach. Just don't rub them with the oil and salt or they'll wilt.*

# SWEET AND SOUR SAUCE

Yield: 2 portions          Preparation Time: 5 minutes          Cook Time: 10 minutes

## INGREDIENTS

1 cup pineapple juice

2 tbsp arrowroot

2 tbsp tomato puree

3 tbsp apple cider vinegar

1 clove garlic crushed

Dash tamari (wheat free soya sauce)

## METHOD

Mix a couple tablespoons of the pineapple juice with the arrowroot and make a thin paste. Keep to one side to use to thicken the sauce at the end.

Gently heat all the other ingredients and simmer for 10 minutes on a really low heat. At the end of the cooking time mix in the arrowroot paste and allow the sauce to thicken.

Pour over any stir-fried dishes.

**NOTES:** *You can add a variety of vegetables and pineapple pieces when simmering the sauce, make it your own.*

# THAI VEGETABLES WITH KONJAC NOODLES

Yield: 3 portions          Preparation Time: 10 minutes          Cook Time: 10 minutes

## INGREDIENTS

2 tbsp coconut oil

1 onion chopped

1 clove garlic crushed

1" ginger grated

1 red pepper sliced

1 handful greens sliced

8 chestnut mushrooms sliced

1 packet Konjac noodles well rinsed

3 cups bean sprouts

2 tbsp toasted sesame oil

1 tsp fish sauce (optional

1 tbsp tamari (wheat free soya sauce)

2 tsp rice vinegar

Small handful of chopped coriander

## METHOD

Gently heat the coconut oil in a large frying pan and fry the onions, garlic and ginger for a couple of minutes until they start to soften. Stirring all the time.

Add the red pepper, greens and mushrooms and fry for another couple of minutes.

The noodles can now be added. Make sure you have rinsed them thoroughly because the smell can be off-putting. Keep stirring for a few minutes and then add the bean sprouts, stirring again.

When the bean sprouts are almost cooked, add the sesame oil, fish sauce, tamari and rice vinegar. Warm through and finally add the chopped coriander to garnish.

Serve on its own or with my Thai Chicken and Aduki Bean Burgers.

**NOTES:** *Konjac noodles are sometimes known as Miracle noodles and are gluten-free and full of resistant starch which feeds the good bacteria in your gut.*

# VEGETABLE FRIED 'RICE'

Yield: 2 portions      Preparation Time: 10 minutes      Cook Time: 10 minutes

## INGREDIENTS

2 tbsp coconut oil

1 medium onion

1 clove garlic crushed

2 medium carrots

1 medium parsnip

1/4 head cauliflower

1/2 cup mixed frozen peas and sweetcorn

1/2 tsp turmeric

1 egg beaten (optional)

3 tbsp toasted sesame oil

1 tbsp tamari (wheat free soya sauce)

1/4 tsp rice vinegar

Ground black pepper

## METHOD

Process all the vegetables, except the peas and sweetcorn in separate batches in a food processor until the same size as a grain of rice. Do not over process.

Heat the oil in a frying pan or wok and fry the onion and garlic for a couple of minutes, stirring frequently. Add the carrots and parsnips and stir-fry for 2 minutes. Add the cauliflower, peas and sweetcorn for another few minutes until cooked to your liking, stirring frequently.

Add the turmeric and black pepper.

If you are using the egg, then add it now and keep stirring until almost cooked.

Finally add the toasted sesame oil, tamari and rice vinegar.

Check the flavours and add more tamari or rice vinegar if necessary.

**NOTES:** *I love to add chillies and peppers too. Vary the vegetables but just remember that the cauliflower, carrot and parsnip are what give the dish its rice-like consistency. You can also use sweet potato.*

# VEGETABLE THORAN

Yield: 2 portions          Preparation Time: 10 minutes          Cook Time: 10 minutes

## INGREDIENTS

1/4 small cabbage (I prefer white)

1 large carrot

1 medium onion

2 tbsp coconut oil

1 tsp mustard seeds

1/2 cup desiccated coconut

1/2 tsp turmeric

Salt and black pepper

## METHOD

Process the vegetables separately in your food processor.

Gently heat the coconut oil in a large pan and add the mustard seeds, cover with a lid for 10 seconds and then add the desiccated coconut.

Mix and cook for 1 minute. Be careful not to burn the mixture.

Add the turmeric, salt, black pepper and stir.

Add your prepared vegetables and gently cook for 5 minutes uncovered, stirring frequently.

NOTES: *Vary the vegetables according to what you have. This Indian dish is fabulous instead of rice with a curry.*

# ABOUT THE AUTHOR

Julie lives in the beautiful South West of England in Torbay, and has done so for the whole of her life. She has two grown-up children, a daughter and son, who regularly come home to try out her new recipes and to spend time with their Mum.

Improve Your Health, Julie's company focuses on helping others to take control of their health via online programmes, retreats, books, blogs and a varied range of Workshops and Masterclasses. She also offers Skype consultations for those who live too far away. In her community, she's known for being an investigative health researcher, speaker at various food and health events and is involved in various community health projects.

Julie has written two other books. 'From Cancer to Clear – my eight eye openers to improve your health'. This is available either on her website or on Amazon. Deliciously Healthy, her first recipe book is available from her website.

Besides learning about health and wellbeing Julie and her partner John, love to go for long walks in the countryside and by the sea. Other interests include cycling, Pilates, and spending time with her friends and family.